My
First Book of
FRENCH

BUSHEL
& PECK
BOOKS

Text copyright © 2022 by Nicolas Jeter and Tony Pesqueira

Published by Bushel & Peck Books, a family-run publishing house in Fresno, California, that believes in uplifting children with the highest standards of art, music, literature, and ideas. Find beautiful books for gifted young minds at www.bushelandpeckbooks.com.

Type set in Providence Sans, Learning Curve, Halewyn, and Chelsea Pro
Artwork licensed from Shutterstock.com.

Bushel & Peck Books is dedicated to fighting illiteracy all over the world. For every book we sell, we donate one to a child in need—book for book. To nominate a school or organization to receive free books, please visit www.bushelandpeckbooks.com.

LCCN: 2022930285
ISBN: 9781638190479

First Edition

Printed in China

10 9 8 7 6 5 4 3 2

800+
Words &
Pictures

My
First Book of

FRENCH

Nicolas
Jeter & Tony
Pesqueira

Contents

good
morning!
bonjour!

FRENCH
BASICS

INTRODUCTION

Bonjour! And welcome to *My First Book of French!* The French language is both beautiful and fascinating, and we hope that this book is a helpful stepping stone as you begin your own French journey. Because this is a beginner's book, we have intentionally kept explanations simple. Our goal is to expose first-time learners to the French language without overwhelming their experience with the nuances of French grammar. As such, think of this book as a first taste of what we hope will become an entire meal of lifetime learning.

Bon appétit!

—Nicolas and Tony

Pronunciation

HOW TO PRONOUNCE EACH LETTER

	HOW TO SAY THE NAME OF THE LETTER	SIMILAR TO ENGLISH SOUND IN:	FRENCH EXAMPLES
a	ah	father	alligator
b	beh	ball	ballon
c	ceh	cat or say	cour, fiancé
d	deh	day	donner
e	uh	elephant	venir
f	eff	father	faire
g	jeh	great	gâteau
h	ache	No English equivalent	The "h" is always soundless in French
i	ee	Greek	ami
j	gee	measure	juger
k	kah	cat	kilo
l	elle	letter	livre
m	emm	Mexico	Méxique
n	enn	North	nord
o	oh	Oh!	orange
p	peh	pillow	parc
q	keu	cub	quarante
r	erre	no English equivalent	**restaurant** (the French "r" is a guttural sound that comes from the throat. Do not "roll" the "r" as in Spanish)

s	esse	sister	**sel** ("s" is almost always silent when it is at the end of the word, as in "tapis"; when between two vowels, "s" has a "z" sound, as in "saisir")
t	teh	turtle	trois
U	ew	No English equivalent	une
V	veh	very	vouloir
W	double veh	very (always a "v" sound)	Wagon (sounds likes "vagon")
X	eeks	explore	maximum
y	ee grek	seek	tyran
z	zed	zoo	zéro

UNIQUE LETTERS IN FRENCH

	SIMILAR TO ENGLISH SOUND IN:	FRENCH EXAMPLES
ç	say	français
è	let	mère
é	say	Été
ê, ë	tell	**Être, Noël** (The dots over the "e" mean that the letter "e" is pronounced separately from the rest of the word, like "No-ël").
i, ï, î	Greek	**Île** (the "i" sound is always the same in French, no matter what symbol is over the letter. Also, when the "i" has dots over it, it is pronounced separately from the rest of the word)

Gender

An important aspect of the French language is the gender of nouns. There are two types: masculine nouns and feminine nouns. The gender of a noun can determine how other parts of speech are written or pronounced. For example:

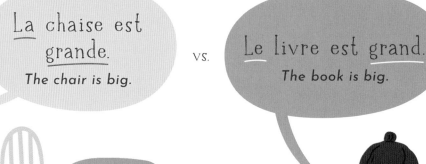

La chaise est grande.

The chair is big.

vs.

Le livre est grand.

The book is big.

Did you spot the differences? Look at the spelling for "grande / grand"—it's different when the object it's describing (the chair vs. the book) is a masculine noun or a feminine one.

This is why, when learning French, it is important to not simply learn nouns but to also learn the gender of the nouns.

LE VS. LA

The main way to tell if a noun is feminine or masculine is whether *le* or *la* is used with the noun. *Le* and *la* both mean the English word "the," but in French, they also indicate the gender of the noun they are modifying. For example, the French word for "apple" is *pomme*. However, *pomme* is a feminine noun in French, so to say "the apple," you say "la pomme."

Le = "the" (for masculine nouns)
La = "the" (for feminine nouns)

But, whether the noun is masculine or feminine, if the noun begins with a vowel, the *le* or *la* gets contracted to just *l'*. For example: *l'orange* ("the orange") or *l'agneau* ("the lamb").

L' = "the" (for all nouns that begin with a vowel or silent "h," whether masculine or feminine)

When a noun is plural, you use *les* for either gender.

Les = "the" (for all plural nouns whether masculine or feminine)

WHAT YOU'LL SEE IN THIS BOOK

Nouns: Definite articles are used as follows: *le* = "the" (masculine); *la* = "the" (feminine); *l'* = *le* or *la* if followed by a vowel or silent "h"; and *les* = "the" for plural nouns, whether masculine or feminine. One of these will accompany each French noun in the book so that the articles can be learned along with the nouns themselves.

Adjectives: A masculine adjective can be made feminine by adding certain letters. In the book, adjectives are given in their masculine form with the feminine additions placed in parentheses. For example, *amical(e)*—which means "friendly"—would be *amical* for masculine nouns and *amicale* for feminine ones.

Look for the following tools to help you get the most out of this section:

🗨 **Example sentences:** See vocabulary in context!

💡 **Language tips:** Get extra insight about the meaning or usage of certain words.

🗼 **Culture cues:** Learn to love the French culture alongside the language!

VOCABULARY

Greetings

Hello, I'm Tony.

Bonjour. Je m'appelle Tony.

good afternoon

bon après-midi

good evening

bonsoir

good night

bonne nuit

💬 It's nice to meet you.
I'm Nicolas.

Enchanté. Je m'appelle Nicolas.

nice to
meet you

enchanté

goodbye

au revoir

I look forward to working
with you

j'ai hâte de travailler avec vous

I am _____.

Je suis _____.

Courtesy

excuse me

excusez-moi

In French, you can use vous or tu to address someone. Usually, it is considered polite to use vous with someone you just met.

I'm sorry

je suis désolé

really?

ah bon?

that's right

c'est vrai

no

non

yes

oui

People

person
la personne

baby
le bébé

toddler
le bambin

child
l'enfant

woman
la femme

girl
la fille

adult
l'adulte

man
le homme

boy
le garçon

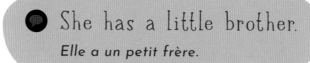

💬 She has a little brother.
Elle a un petit frère.

people
les gens

female
femelle

male
male

friendly
amical(e)

friends
les amis

21

Personal Pronouns

HELLO
MY NAME IS
Mme Unetelle

↑
⋯ name
le nom

Mr.
Monsieur

Mrs.
Madame

Ms.
Mademoiselle

I
je

me
moi

you
vous / tu

She is Mrs. So-and-So.
Elle est Madame Unetelle.

everybody
tout le monde

they
ils / elles

them
eux

we / us
nous

he
il

she
elle

Land

land
la terre

mountain range
la chaîne de montagnes

the world
le monde

geography
la géographie

landscape
la paysage

plain
la plaine

💬 I climbed a mountain.
J'ai gravi une montagne.

peak
le sommet

mountain
la montagne

hill
la colline

The tallest mountain in France is named Mont Blanc and measures 15,774 feet!

stone
la pierre

Earth
la Terre

rock / boulder
la roche

SOIL

ground / soil
le sol

25

Water

water
l'eau

waterfall
la cascade

ocean
l'océan

beach
la plage

sand
le sable

sea
la mer

coast
la côte

lake
le lac

river
la rivière

English Channel

La Manche

France

La France

Massif
Central

*Le Massif
Central*

 France is commonly
called "The Hexagon"
(*l'Hexagone*) because
it has six sides. Three
of those sides are
bordered by water.

LILLE

ROUEN

Seine

Paris

STRASBOURG

BREST

RENNES

ORLÉANS

NANTES

Loire

TOURS

DIJON

LIMOGES

LYON

Alps

Les Alpes

BORDEAUX

GRENOBLE

Garonne

Rhône

MONTPELLIER

NICE

TOULOUSE

MARSEILLE

AJACC

Pyrenees

Les Pyrénées

France has
seven mountain
ranges!

island

l'île

Mediterranean Sea

La Mer Méditerranée

Face

face
la figure

In French, one refers to parts of the body with "the" instead of "my" or "your."

Je me brosse les dents.
I brush my teeth.

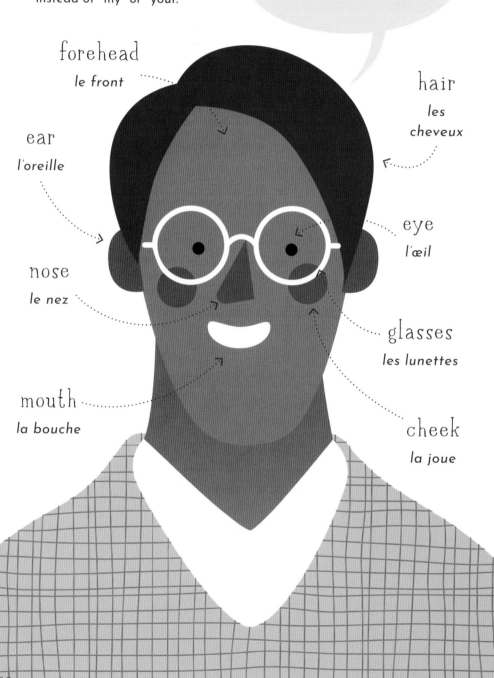

forehead
le front

ear
l'oreille

nose
le nez

mouth
la bouche

hair
les cheveux

eye
l'œil

glasses
les lunettes

cheek
la joue

Body
body
le corps

stature / height
la taille

head
la tête

wrist
le poignet

hand
la main

neck
le cou

shoulder
l'épaule

finger
le doigt

arm
le bras

heart
le cœur

stomach
l'estomac

waist
la taille

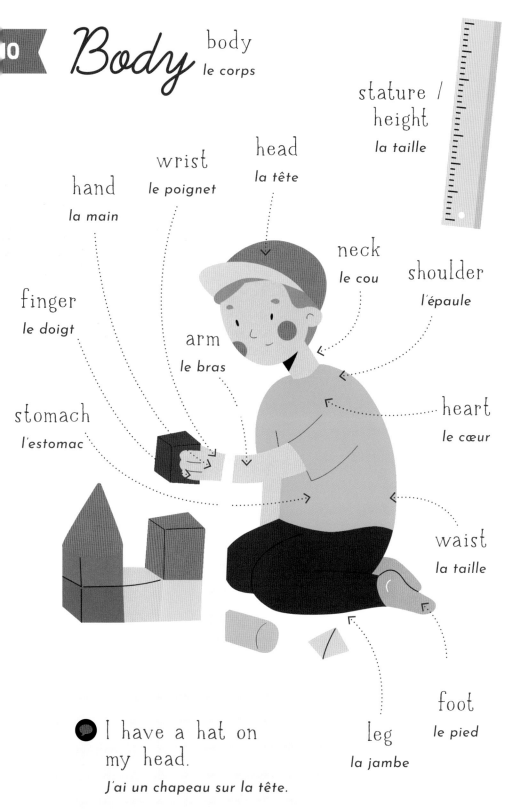

foot
le pied

leg
la jambe

● I have a hat on my head.
J'ai un chapeau sur la tête.

Clothing

Nous portons des vêtements très chics.

We are wearing very cool clothes.

clothing
les vêtements

to wear
porter

necktie
la cravate

suit
le costume

dress
la robe

pants
les pantalons

coat
le manteau

shoe
la chaussure

hat
le chapeau

raincoat
l'imperméable

T-shirt
le tee-shirt

shirt
la chemise

sock
la chaussette

skirt
la jupe

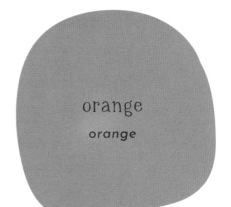

Colors

color
la couleur

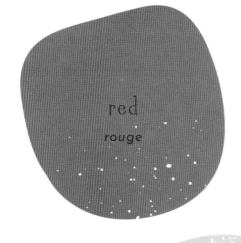

red
rouge

orange
orange

yellow
jaune

green
vert

blue
bleu

purple
violet

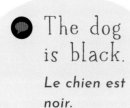

The dog is black.
Le chien est noir.

white
blanc

black
noir

gray
gris

gold
or

silver
argent

brown
brun

pink
rose

Opposites

small
petit

big
grand

heavy
lourd

light
léger

hot
chaud

cold
froid

tall
grand

You will notice that the French words for "small" and "short" are the same, and the words for "big" and "tall" are the same.

short
petit

full
plein

empty
vide

dirty
sale

clean
nette

Shapes

circle
le cercle

square
le carré

rectangle
le rectangle

triangle
le triangle

hexagon
le hexagone

pentagon
le pentagone

octagon
l'octagone

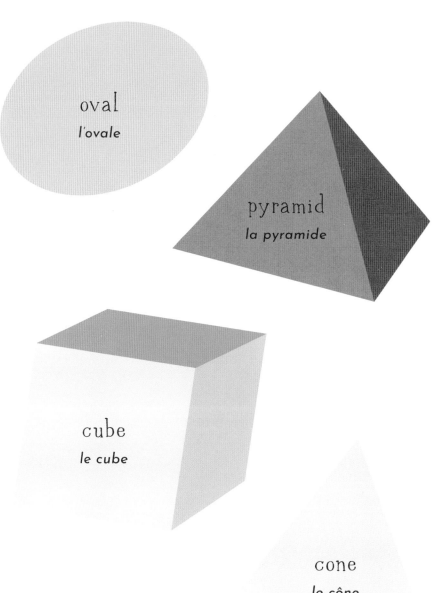

oval
l'ovale

pyramid
la pyramide

cube
le cube

cone
le cône

sphere
la sphère

My Family

grandma
la grand-mère

grandpa
le grand-père

dad
le papa

mom
la maman

parents
les parents

son
le fils

YOU

daughter
la fille

family
la famille

Elle a un petit frère.
She has a little brother.

uncle
l'oncle

aunt
la tante

sisters
les sœurs

brothers
les frères

big
sister

*la grande
sœur*

little
sister

*la petite
sœur*

big
brother

*le grand
frère*

little
brother

*le petit
frère*

Directions

directions
les directions

map
la carte

north
le nord

compass
la boussole

west
l'ouest

east
l'est

south
le sud

far / distant
loin

Space

planet
la planète

space
l'espace

universe
l'univers

star
l'étoile

comet
la comète

43

Weather

weather
le temps

a
beautiful
day
*une belle
journée*

cloud
le nuage

lightning
la foudre

thunder
le tonnere

storm
l'orage

snow
la neige

humid
humide

hail

la grêle

hurricane

l'ouragan

tornado

la tornade

rainbow

l'arc-en-ciel

rain

la pluie

wind

le vent

Plants

plants
les plantes

🗨 I love to visit the forest.

J'adore visiter la forêt.

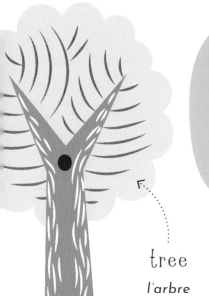

tree
l'arbre

woods / grove
les bois / le bosquet

grass
l'herbe

bush
l'arbuste, le buisson

forest
la forêt

citrus
l'agrume

leaf
la feuille

wisteria
la glycine

trunk
le tronc

flower
la fleur

pot
le pot de fleurs

greenhouse
la serre

rose
la rose

herbs
les herbes

Animals

animal
l'animal

cow
la vache

cat
le chat

pig
le cochon

deer
le cerf

dog
le chien

monkey
le singe

fox
le renard

alligator
l'alligator

bear
l'ours

polar bear
l'ours blanc

panda
le panda

penguin
le manchot

elephant
l'éléphant

lion
le lion

49

bird
l'oiseau

sparrow
le moineau

chicken
le poulet

crane
la grue

crow
le corbeau

insect
l'insecte

bee
l'abeille

butterfly
le papillon

frog
la grenouille

salmon
le saumon

carp
la carpe

tuna
le thon

turtle
la tortue

snake
le serpent

the four seasons
les quatre saisons

season
la saison

Spring
le printemps

Summer
l'été

Autumn
l'automne

Winter
l'hiver

L'été, c'est ma saison préférée.
Summer is my favorite season.

year
l'année

calendar
le calendrier

this year
cette année

last year
l'année dernière

next year
l'année prochaine

every year
chaque année

53

22

Months

month

le mois

January

janvier

February

février

March

mars

April

avril

May

mai

June

juin

this
month
ce mois-ci

next
month
le mois
prochain

last
month
le mois
dernier

every
month
chaque
mois

July
juillet

August
août

September
septembre

October
octobre

November
novembre

December
décembre

Days of the Week

days of the week
les jours de la semaine

week
la semaine

this week
cette semaine

next week
la semaine prochaine

every week
toutes les semaines

last week
la semaine dernière

weekday
le jour de la semaine

workday
la journée de travail

Monday *lundi*	Tuesday *mardi*
1	2
8	9
15	16
22	23
29	30

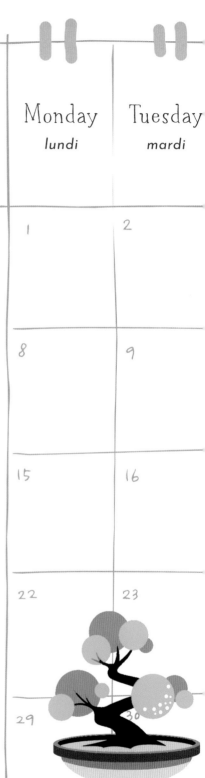

24

Time

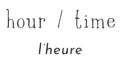

onze heures (11 am)
vingt-trois heures (11 pm)

hour / time
l'heure

dix heures (10 am)
vingt-deux heures (10 pm)

neuf heures (9 am)
vingt et une heures (9 pm)

morning / AM
le matin

huit heures (8 am)
vingt heures (8 pm)

afternoon / PM
l'après-midi

sept heures (7 am)
dix-neuf heures (7 pm)

midi/douze heures (noon / 12 pm)
minuit/vingt-quatre heures
(midnight / 12 am)

une heure (1 am)
treize heures (1 pm)

deux heures (2 am)
quatorze heures (2 pm)

trois heures (3 am)
quinze heures (3 pm)

quatre heures (4 am)
seize heures (4 pm)

clock
l'horloge

cinq heures (5 am)
dix-sept heures (5 pm)

six heures (6 am)
ix-huit heures (6 pm)

59

25

Time of Day

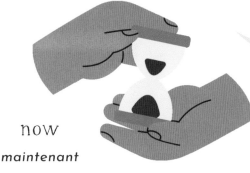

now

maintenant

morning

le matin

noon / midday

le midi

evening

le soir

evening /
night

la soirée

night

la nuit

midnight

le minuit

● Je vais chez le médecin à midi.

I am going to the doctor at noon.

What time is it?

Il est quelle heure?

hourglass
le sablier

yesterday
hier

today
aujourd'hui

tomorrow
demain

every day
tous les jours

every night
toutes les nuits

every morning
tous les matins

sometimes
parfois

26

Countries

parliament
le Parlement

Senate
le Sénat

National Assembly
l'Assemblée Nationale

prime minister
le premier ministre

country
le pays

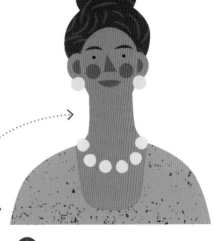

France is governed by a president.

HAUTS DE FRANCE
LILLE
ROUEN
NORMANDIE
PARIS
ILE DE FRANCE
GRAND EST
STRASBOURG
BRETAGNE
RENNES
PAYS DE LA LOIRE
ORLEANS
NANTES
CENTRE VAL DE LOIRE
DIJON
BOURGOGNE FRANCHE COMTE
LYON
NOUVELLE AQUITAINE
AUVERGNE RHONE ALPES
BORDEAUX
OCCITANIE
PROVENCE ALPES CÔTE D'AZUR
TOULOUSE
MARSEILLE
CORSIKA
AJACCIO

region
la région

France is divided into eighteen regions, five of which are spread all over the world: Guadeloupe, Martinique, French Guiana, Mayotte, Réunion, and Corsica.

● You want to
visit France.

*Vous voulez visiter la
France.*

president
le président / la présidente

Spain
l'Espagne

Germany
l'Allemagne

China
la Chine

Mexico
le Mexique

Brazil
le Brésil

United
States
*les Etats-Unis
d'Amérique*

Canada
le Canada

England
/ United
Kingdom
*l'Angleterre, le
Royaume-Uni*

Urban and Rural

zoo
le zoo

suburb
la banlieue

city
la ville

bank
la banque

hospital
l'hôpital

city hall
la mairie

art museum
le musée d'art

library
la bibliothèque

village
le village

farm
la ferme

countryside
la campagne

65

Construction

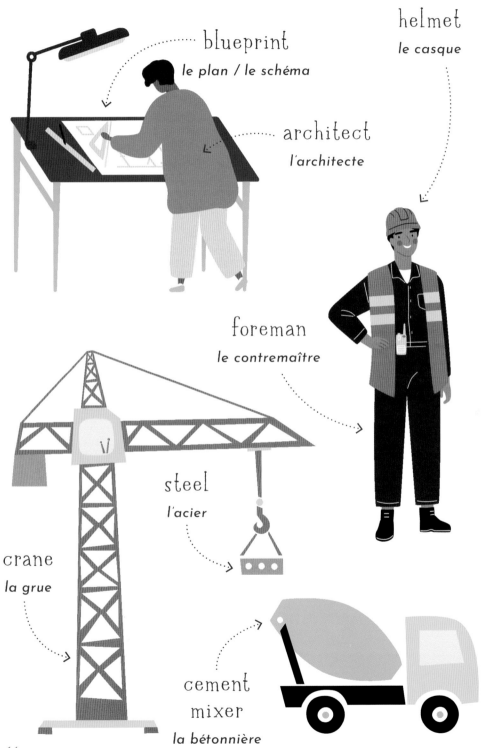

blueprint
le plan / le schéma

helmet
le casque

architect
l'architecte

foreman
le contremaître

steel
l'acier

crane
la grue

cement
mixer
la bétonnière

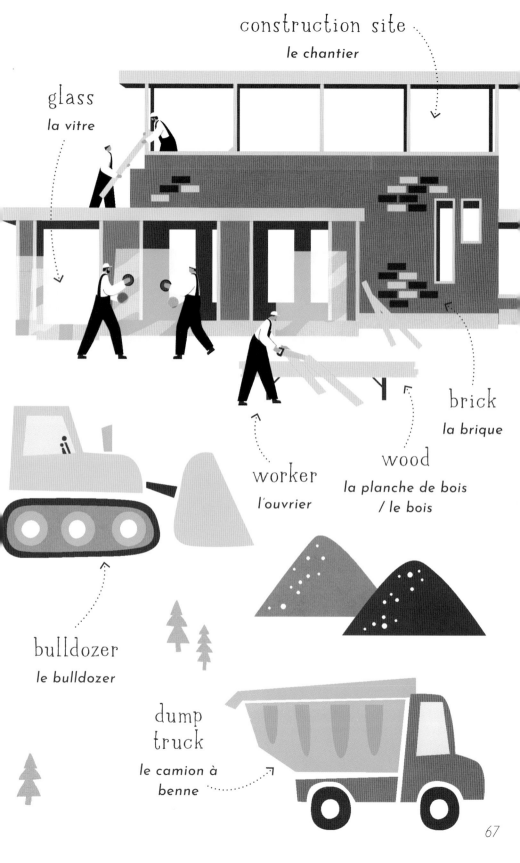

construction site
le chantier

glass
la vitre

brick
la brique

wood
*la planche de bois
/ le bois*

worker
l'ouvrier

bulldozer
le bulldozer

dump
truck
*le camion à
benne*

67

29

Transportation

traffic
la circulation

transportation
le transport

bus stop
l'arrêt de bus

**signal /
traffic light**
*le feu de
circulation*

street
la rue

bus
le bus

taxi
le taxi

car
la voiture

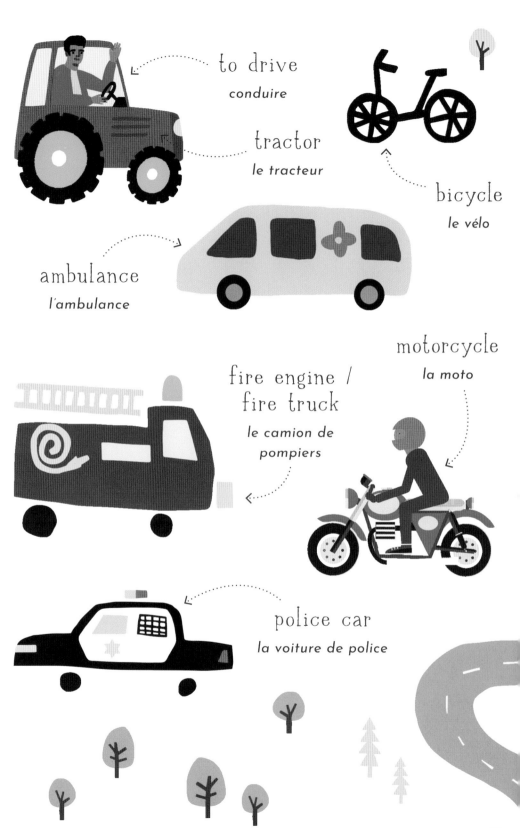

to drive
conduire

tractor
le tracteur

bicycle
le vélo

ambulance
l'ambulance

motorcycle
la moto

fire engine /
fire truck
le camion de pompiers

police car
la voiture de police

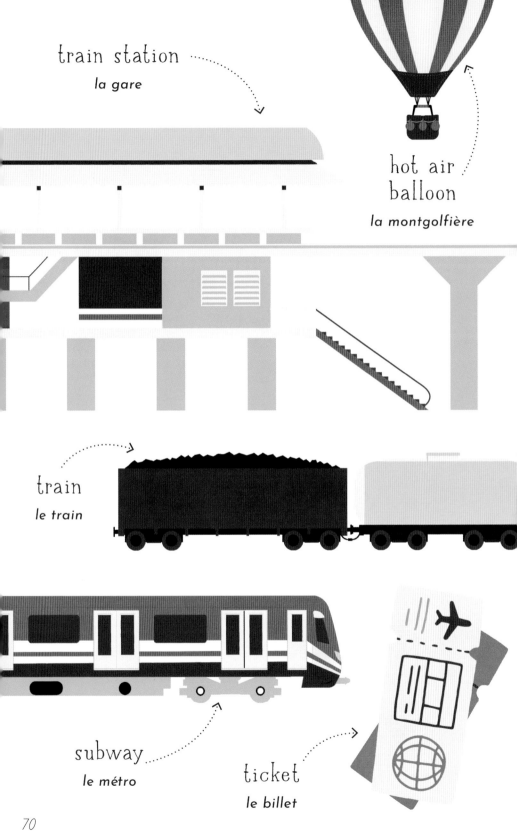

train station
la gare

hot air balloon
la montgolfière

train
le train

subway
le métro

ticket
le billet

bullet train

le train à grande vitesse

The bullet trains can travel up to 300 km/h (186 miles per hour)!

airport

l'aéroport

airplane

l'avion

boat

le bateau

harbor

le havre

30

Travel

inn
l'auberge

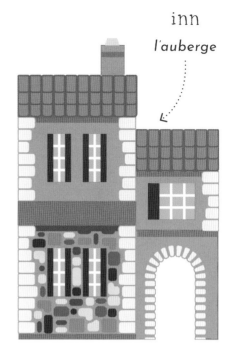

trip /
journey
le voyage

vacation
les vacances

hotel room
*la chambre
d'hôtel*

hotel
l'hôtel

passport
le passeport

PASSPORT

overseas /
abroad
l'étranger

> 💬 Goodbye! We'll see each other again in two weeks.
>
> *Au revoir! On se voit d'ici à deux semaines.*

travel agency
l'agence de voyage

luggage
le bagage

to reserve
réserver

LE DÉPART	L'ARRIVÉE
departure	arrival
le départ	*l'arrivée*

73

31

Around Paris

monument

le monument

Eiffel Tower

La Tour Eiffel

bookseller

le libraire

In Paris, booksellers called *bouquinistes* like to sell books along the River Seine.

museum

la musée

Le Musée du Louvre used to be the French palace. Today, it's home to the *Mona Lisa*.

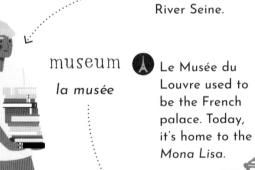

palace

le palais

The Palais de Versailles used to a hunting lodge before King Louis XIV made it his home.

café

le café

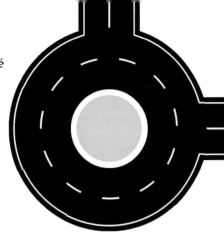

garden

le jardin

bench

le banc

cathedral

la cathédrale

The Cathedral of Notre Dame is more than 850 years old.

bridge

le pont

Museum

statue
la statue

column
la colonne / le pilier

tourists
les touristes

gallery
la galerie

dinosaur
le dinosaure

skeleton
le squelette

exhibit
l'exposition

artifact
l'artéfact

tour guide
le guide touristique

fossil
le fossile

Shopping

shop
la boutique

store
le magasin

how much is it?
Cela coûte combien?

money
l'argent

to buy
acheter

customer
le consommateur

euro
l'euro

dollar
le dollar

France is a part of the European Union, so the French use *euros* for money. Before using the euro, the French used the *franc*.

● I often go to the bookstore to find good books.

Je vais souvent à la librairie pour trouver de bons livres.

cheap / inexpensive
pas cher

expensive
cher

convenience store
le dépanneur

supermarket
le supermarché

bookstore
la librairie

bakery
la boulangerie

department store
le grand magasin

34

Home

house
la maison

window
la fenêtre

chimney
la cheminée

roof
le toit

wall
le mur

apartments
les appartements

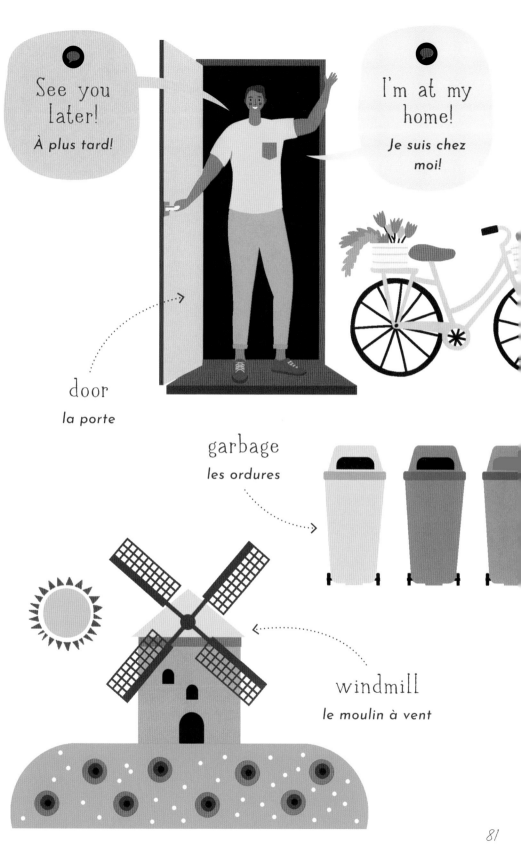

See you later!
À plus tard!

I'm at my home!
Je suis chez moi!

door
la porte

garbage
les ordures

windmill
le moulin à vent

81

35

Bedroom

bed
le lit

room / bedroom
la chambre

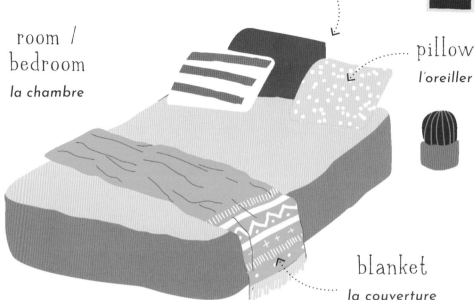

pillow
l'oreiller

blanket
la couverture

to go to bed
aller au lit

hanger
le cintre

wardrobe
l'armoire

I have to clean my room.
Je dois ranger ma chambre.

dark
sombre

bright
brillant(e)

light
la lumière

to sleep
dormir

to awaken /
to wake up
se réveiller

turn on
allumer

turn off
éteindre

mirror
le miroir

switch
le interrupteur

83

Bathroom

to wash oneself
se laver

shower
la douche

toilet
room
*la salle de
toilette*

bath
le bain

bathroom
*la salle de
bain*

toilet
la toilette

to brush
(teeth)
brosser

● Mon petit frère apprend
à aller aux toilettes.
*My little brother is learning to use
the toilet.*

sink
l'évier

Kitchen

kitchen
la cuisine

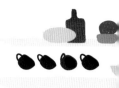

microwave oven
le micro-onde

refrigerator
le réfrigérateur /
le frigo

flame
la flamme

stove
le poêle

oven
le four

table
la table

chair
la chaise

School

school
l'école

kindergarten
l'école maternelle

elementary
school
(grades 1-6)
l'école primaire

middle school (grades 8-9)
le collège / l'école intermédiaire

high school
(grades 10-11)
le lycée

**uniform /
school uniform**
l'uniforme

student
l'étudiant

teacher
l'enseignant

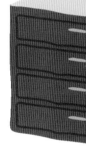

In France, students start school as young as three years old.

university
l'université

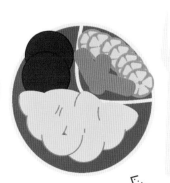

school lunch
le repas scolaire

39

Classroom

classroom
la salle de classe /
la salle de cours

blackboard
le tableau noir

test
*l'examen,
le test*

a b c
d e f g h
i j k l m
n o p q r
s t u v w
x y z é è

desk
le bureau

pencil
le crayon

pen
le stylo

paper
le papier

It's important to study well to pass the exam.

Il faut bien étudier pour réussir à l'examen.

to study
étudier

book
le livre

to write
écrire

textbook
le manuel / le manuel scolaire

schoolbag
le sac à dos

page
la page

homework
le devoir

40

Subjects

education
l'éducation

class
le cours

school
subject
la matière

lesson
la leçon

language
la langue

mathemathics
la mathématique

French language
(school subject
for native
students)
le cours de français

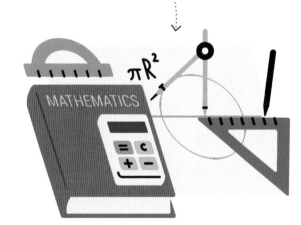

English
(language)
le cours d'anglais

grammar
la grammaire

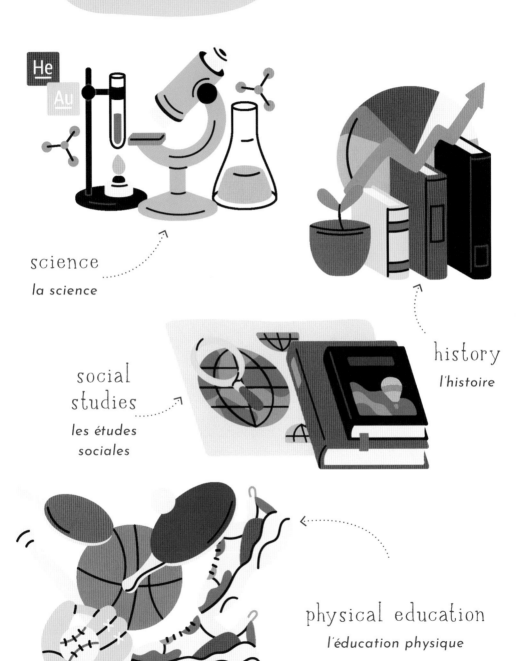

I love studying!
J'adore étudier!

science
la science

history
l'histoire

social
studies
les études sociales

physical education
l'éducation physique

41

Science

experiment
l'expérience

scientist
le scientifique

hypothesis
l'hypothèse

astronomy
l'astronomie

physics
la physique

laboratory
le laboratoire

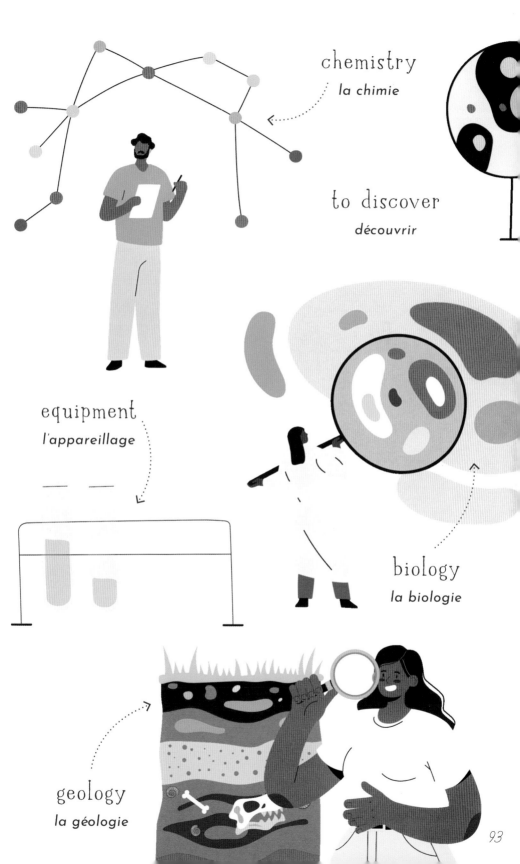

chemistry
la chimie

to discover
découvrir

equipment
l'appareillage

biology
la biologie

geology
la géologie

93

42

Learning

to learn
apprendre

vocabulary
le vocabulaire

to teach
enseigner

word
le mot

question
la question

correct
correct(e)

to understand
comprendre

to study
étudier

to memorize
mémoriser

to forget
oublier

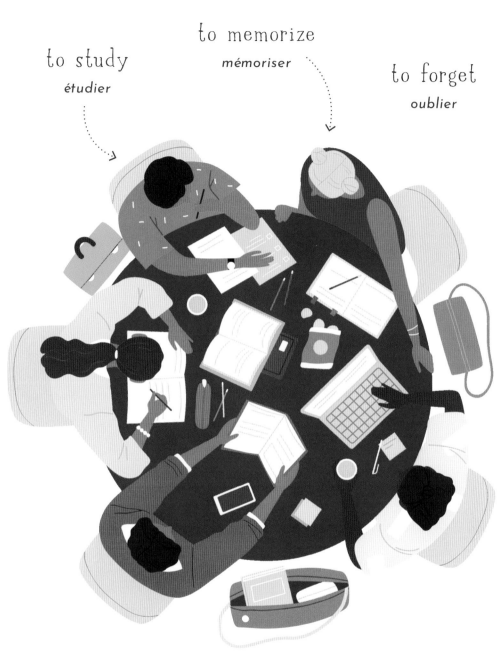

difficult
difficile

easy
facile

study group
le groupe d'étude

43

Health

health
la santé

injury
la blessure

pain
la douleur

healthy
sain(e)

spirit
l'esprit

safe
sûr

illness
la maladie

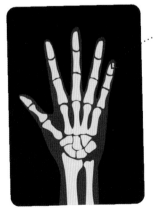

bone
l'os

headache
le mal de tête

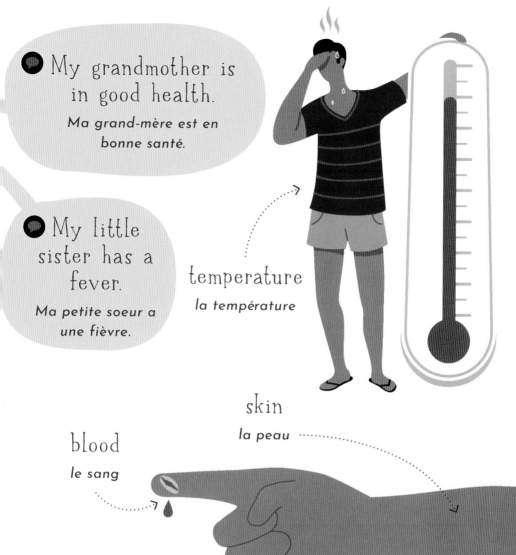

My grandmother is in good health.

Ma grand-mère est en bonne santé.

My little sister has a fever.

Ma petite soeur a une fièvre.

temperature

la température

skin

la peau

blood

le sang

common cold

le rhume

cough

la toux

fever

la fièvre

44

Work

to work
travailler

part-time job
l'emploi à temps partiel

meeting room
la salle de réunion

company
l'entreprise

office
le bureau

employee
l'employé

> I finally have free time! I will relax on the couch with my favorite book.
>
> *Enfin du temps libre! Je me détendrai sur le canapé avec mon livre préféré.*

to relax
se détendre

day off
le jour de congé

police officer
l'officier de police

lawyer
l'avocat

nurse
l'infirmière

doctor
le docteur

45

Hobbies

to hike
marcher à pied

hobby / pastime
le passe-temps

yarn
le fil

to read
lire

to knit
tricoter

movie theater
le cinéma

animation
l'animation

movie
le film

game
le jeu

fun
l'amusement

to play
jouer

to sing
chanter

voice
la voix

to dance
danser

gardening
la guitare

guitar
la guitare

piano
le piano

101

Music

music
la musique

composer
le compositeur

flute
la flûte

musician
le musicien

harp
la harpe

saxophone
le saxophone

tambourine
le tambourin

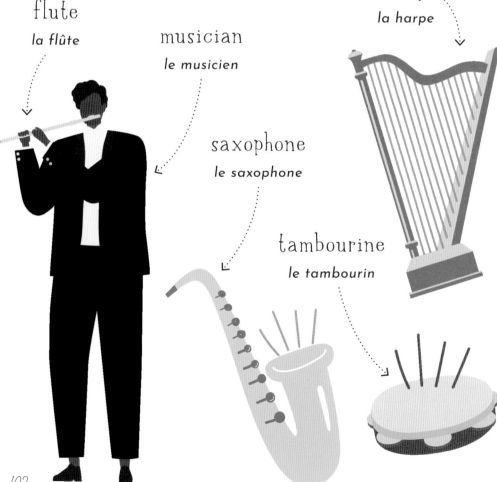

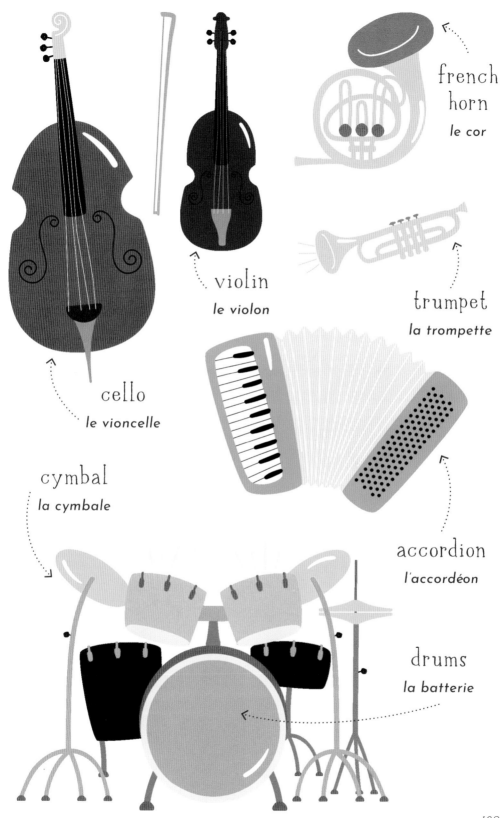

french
horn
le cor

violin
le violon

trumpet
la trompette

cello
le vioncelle

cymbal
la cymbale

accordion
l'accordéon

drums
la batterie

103

47

Art

potter
le potier

ceramics
la céramique

easel
le chevalet

painting
la peinture

ink
l'encre

photography
la photographie

charcoal
le fusain

pastel
le pastel

watercolor
l'aquerelle

brushes
les pinceaux

eraser
la gomme

oil paint
la peinture à l'huile

model
la maquette

tape
le ruban

artist
l'artiste

105

sports
les sports

basketball
le basket

soccer
le football

athlete
l'athlète

The biggest sport in France is soccer, but basketball is growing in popularity.

baseball
le baseball

team
l'équipe

victory
la victoire

football
le football américain

defeat
la défaite

player
le joueur

to exercise
faire de l'exercice

to walk
marcher

to practice
pratiquer / s'entraîner

to run
courir

ping pong / table tennis
le ping-pong

match
le match

tennis
le tennis

volleyball
le volley

swimming
la natation

107

Holidays

holiday
la fête

birthday
l'anniversaire

Ramadan
Le Ramadan

Easter
Les Pâques

All Saint's Day
La Fête de la Toussaint

On Toussaint, the French gather at cemeteries to place flowers at the graves of their loved ones.

Bastille Day
La Fête Nationale française / le 14 juillet

Bastille Day celebrates the beginning of the French Revolution on July 14, 1789.

Halloween
La Fête d'Halloween

Armistice Day
L'Armistice

Father's Day
La Fête des Pères

Mother's Day
La Fête des Mères

Mardi Gras
Le Mardi Gras

Christmas Eve
La veille de Noël

Christmas
Le Noël

Valentine's Day
Le Jour de Saint-Valentin

New Year's Day
Le Nouvel An

communication
la communication

to speak
parler

to say
dire

cell phone
le téléphone portable

allô?
hello?

make a phone call
téléphoner

telephone
le téléphone

radio
la radio

TV
la télé

television
la télévision

Internet
l'Internet

computer
l'ordinateur

post office
le bureau de poste

mailbox /
postbox
la boîte aux lettres

postcard
la carte postale

mail
le courrier

letter
la lettre

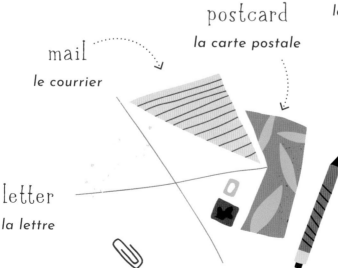

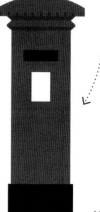

111

51

Fairy Tales

story
l'histoire

queen
la reine

once upon a time
il était une fois

king
le roi

tale
le conte

castle
le château

prince
le prince

princess
la princesse

knight
le chevalier

dragon
le dragon

cottage
le chalet

witch
la sorcière

legend
la légende

happily
ever after
*heureux pour
toujours*

wizard
l'assistant

Meals

meal
la farine / le repas

breakfast
le petit-déjeuner

lunch
le déjeuner

food
la nourriture

The French like to take their time while eating, and meals can sometimes even last a few hours, especially during the holidays.

dinner
le dîner

dessert
le dessert

to eat
manger

Drink

to drink
boire

tea
le thé

hot
chocolate
le chocolat chaud

milk
le lait

lemonade
la limonade

coffee
le café

drink /
beverage
la boisson

soda
le soda

vending
machine
*le distributeur
automatique*

juice
le jus

Fruits

fruit
le fruit

apples
la pomme

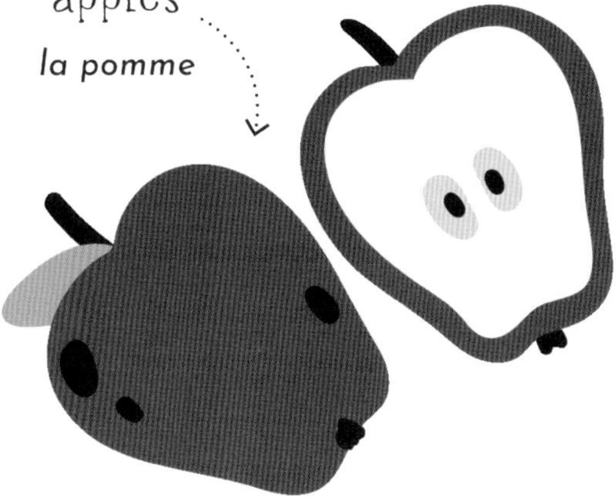

peach
la pêche

pear
la poire

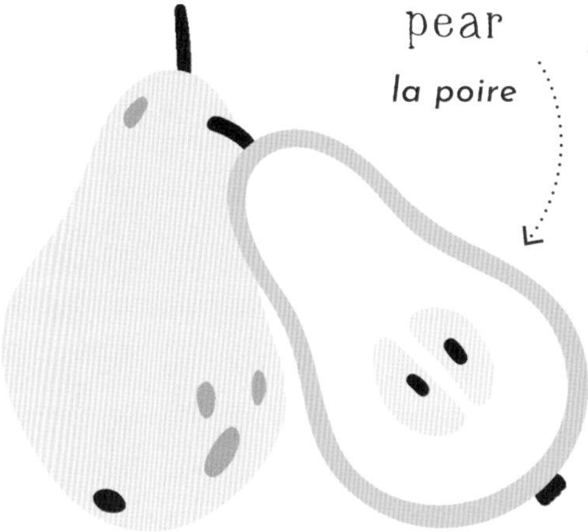

orange
l'orange

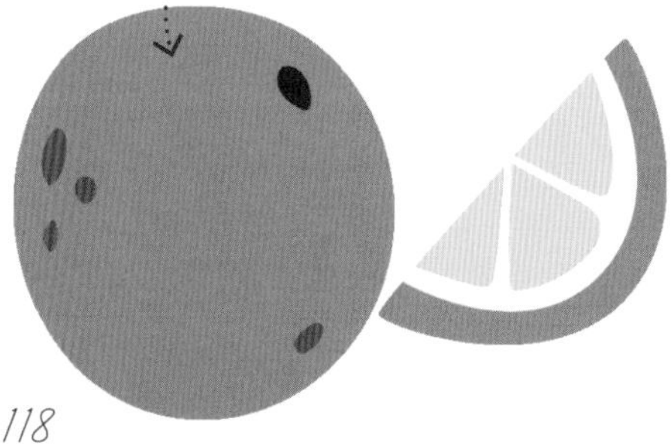

pineapple
l'ananas

strawberry
la fraise

grape
le raisin

fig
la figue

melon
le melon

watermelon
la pastèque

banana
la banane

apricot
le abricot

55

Vegetables

vegetable
le légume

carrot
la carotte

tomato
la tomate

eggplant
l'aubergine

green onion
l'oignon vert

onion
l'oignon

garlic
l'ail

potato
la pomme de terre

broccoli
le brocoli

sweet potato
la patate douce

celery
le céleri

lettuce
la laitue

mushroom
le champignon

cabbage
le chou

121

Protein and Dairy

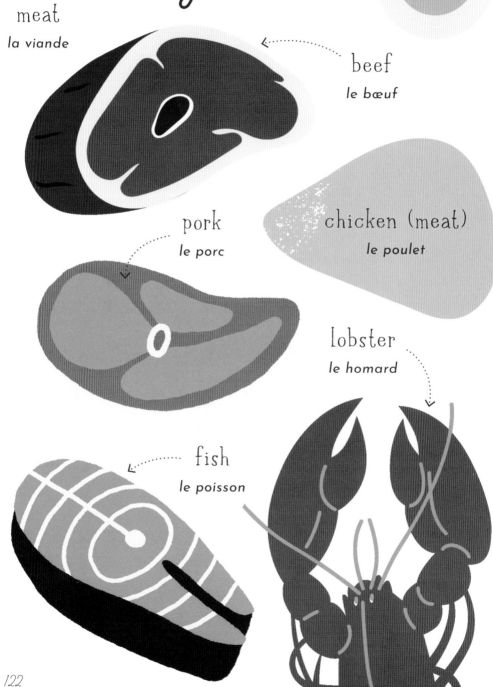

meat
la viande

beef
le bœuf

pork
le porc

chicken (meat)
le poulet

lobster
le homard

fish
le poisson

mussels
les moules

eggs
les œufs

butter
le beurre

France has over 1,000 varieties of cheese!

dairy products
les produits laitiers

cheese
le fromage

yogurt
le yaourt

cream
la crème

57

Dessert

madeleine

la madeleine

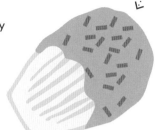

pastry

la pâtisserie

 Pastries are important to daily life in France. Bakers make pastries fresh every day!

eclair

l'éclair

sweet

amai

cookie

le biscuit

chocolate

le chocolat

cake

le gateau

● Refreshing! I love ice cream.
Rafraîchisant! J'adore la glace.

ice cream
la glace

tart
la tarte

macaron
le macaron

125

58

Cooking

Magnificent! This tastes very good.

Magnifique! Ça goûte très bon.

to cook
cuisiner

to bake
cuire

chef
le chef

flavor
le goût

restaurant
le restaurant

ingredient
l'ingrédient

sugar
le sucre

knife
le couteau

cup
la tasse

fork
la fourchette

salt
le sel

spoon
la cuillère

pepper
le poivre noir

recipe
la recette

frying pan / skillet
la poêle

dish towel
le torchon à vaisselle

saucepan / pot
le casserole ou le pot

cutting board
la planche à découper

127

59

Cuisine

ratatouille
la ratatouille

A dish of stewed vegetables, usually including onion, eggplant, and zucchini.

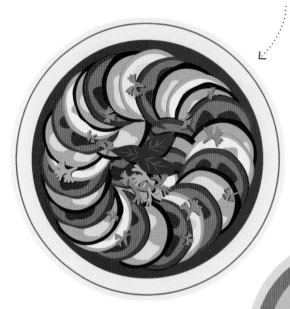

french onion soup
la soupe à l'oignon

A delicious soup made from slow-cooked onions and beef broth and usually topped with croutons and melted cheese.

beef stew
le bœuf bourguignon

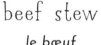 A slow-cooked beef stew with hearty vegetables and rich gravy.

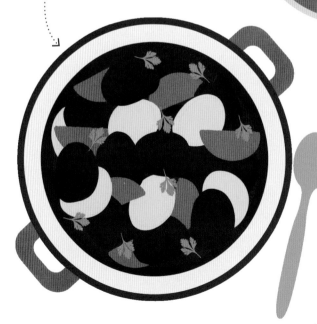

french bread
la baguette

niçoise salad

la salade niçoise

🗼 A traditional salad made from greens, olives, eggs, and anchovies.

cassoulet

le cassoulet

🗼 A mix of white beans and various meats (like pork and sausage) that are slowly stewed together.

croissant

le croissant

cheese and meat board

la charcuterie

60

Numbers

1

number

les numéros

← one

un

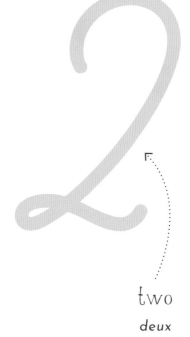

two

deux

3

three ⋯⋯

trois

five

cinq

4

← four

quatre

six
six

seven
sept

eight
huit

nine
neuf

ten
dix

Bigger Numbers

11	eleven	onze
12	twelve	douze
13	thirteen	treize
14	fourteen	quatorze
15	fifteen	quinze
16	sixteen	seize
17	seventeen	dix-sept
18	eighteen	dix-huit
19	nineteen	dix-neuf
20	twenty	vingt
30	thirty	trente
40	forty	quarante
50	fifty	cinquante
60	sixty	soixante
70	seventy	soixante-dix
80	eighty	quatre-vingts
90	ninety	quatre-vingt-dix
100	hundred	cent
200	two hundred	deux-cents
300	three hundred	trois-cents
400	four hundred	quatre-cents
500	five hundred	cinq-cents

600	six hundred	six-cents
700	seven hundred	sept-cents
800	eight hundred	huit-cents
900	nine hundred	neuf-cents
1,000	thousand	mille
2,000	two thousand	deux-mille
3,000	three thousand	trois-mille
4,000	four thousand	quatre-mille
5,000	five thousand	cinq-mille
6,000	six thousand	six-mille
7,000	seven thousand	sept-mille
8,000	eight thousand	huit-mille
9,000	nine thousand	neuf-mille
10,000	ten thousand	dix-mille
20,000	twenty thousand	vingt-mille
30,000	thirty thousand	trente-mille
40,000	forty thousand	quarante-mille
50,000	fifty thousand	cinquante-mille
60,000	sixty thousand	soixante-mille
70,000	seventy thousand	soixante-dix-mille
80,000	eighty thousand	quatre-vingt-mille
90,000	ninety thousand	quatre-vingt-dix-mille

62

Making Numbers

💡 As in English, large numbers in French are just combinations of smaller numbers.

345

three hundred + forty + five

trois-cents + *quarante* + *cinq*

three hundred forty-five

trois-cent-quarante-cinq

2,345

two thousand three hundred forty-five

deux-mille-trois-cent-quarante-cinq

12,345

twelve thousand three hundred forty-five

douze-mille-trois-cent-quarante-cinq

Word Index

office / 98
oil paint / 105
once upon a time / 112
one / 130
onion / 120
orange / 32
orange / 118
oval / 37
oven / 85
overseas / abroad / 72
page / 89
pain / 96
painting / 104
palace / 74
panda / 49
pants / 31
paper / 88
parents / 38
parliament / 62
part-time job / 98
passport / 72
pastel / 104
pastry / 124
peach / 118
peak / 25
pear / 118
pen / 88
pencil / 88
penguin / 49
pentagon / 36
people / 21
pepper / 127
person / 20
photography / 104
physical education / 91
physics / 92
piano / 101
pig / 48
pillow / 82
pineapple / 118

ping pong / table tennis / 107
pink / 33
plain / 24
planet / 42
plants / 46
player / 106
please / 18
polar bear / 49
police car / 69
police officer / 99
pork / 122
postcard / 111
post office / 111
pot / 47
potato / 120
potter / 104
president / 63
prime minister / 62
prince / 112
princess / 112
purple / 32
pyramid / 37
Pyrenees / 27
queen / 112
question / 94
radio / 111
rain / 45
rainbow / 45
raincoat / 31
Ramadan / 108
ratatouille / 128
really? / 19
recipe / 127
rectangle / 36
red / 32
refrigerator / 85
region / 62
restaurant / 126
right / 41

river / 26
rock /
boulder / 25
roof / 80
room / bedroom / 82
rose / 47
safe / 96
salmon / 51
salt / 127
sand / 26
Saturday / 57
saucepan / pot / 127
saxophone / 102
school / 86
schoolbag / 89
school lunch / 87
school subject / 90
science / 91
scientist / 92
sea / 26
season / 52
See you later! / 81
Senate / 62
September / 55
seven / 131
she / 23
shirt / 31
shoe / 31
shop / 78
short / 35
shoulder / 29
shower / 84
signal / traffic light / 68
silver / 33
sink / 84
sisters / 39
six / 131
skeleton / 77
skin / 97
skirt / 31

ABOUT THE AUTHORS

Nicolas Jeter lived in France prior to beginning his writing career and is fluent in French. His debut children's book, *The Girl and the Cathedral: The Story of Notre Dame de Paris*, was published in 2020. He practices tax law in Dallas, Texas.

Tony Pesqueira lives near Houston, Texas. His passions include being a husband and father to his wife and two sons, and all things soccer. Tony is fluent in English, Spanish, French, and Portuguese, and works as an interpreter and translator for these languages in the tech industry. His love for French was born while living in Montreal, Canada, for two years. This is his first children's book.

BUSHEL
& PECK
BOOKS

ABOUT BUSHEL & PECK BOOKS

Bushel & Peck Books is a children's publishing house with a special mission. Through our Book-for-Book Promise™, we donate one book to kids in need for every book we sell. Our beautiful books are given to kids through schools, libraries, local neighborhoods, shelters, nonprofits, and also to many selfless organizations that are working hard to make a difference. So thank you for purchasing this book! Because of you, another book will make its way into the hands of a child who needs it most.

NOMINATE A SCHOOL OR ORGANIZATION TO RECEIVE FREE BOOKS

Do you know a school, library, or organization that could use some free books for their kids? We'd love to help! Please fill out the nomination form on our website, and we'll do everything we can to make something happen.

www.bushelandpeckbooks.com/pages/
nominate-a-school-or-organization

If you liked this book, please leave a review online at your favorite retailer. Honest reviews spread the word about Bushel & Peck—and help us make better books, too!